Cook with aba

CU0854614B

drizzleanddip.com

Sam

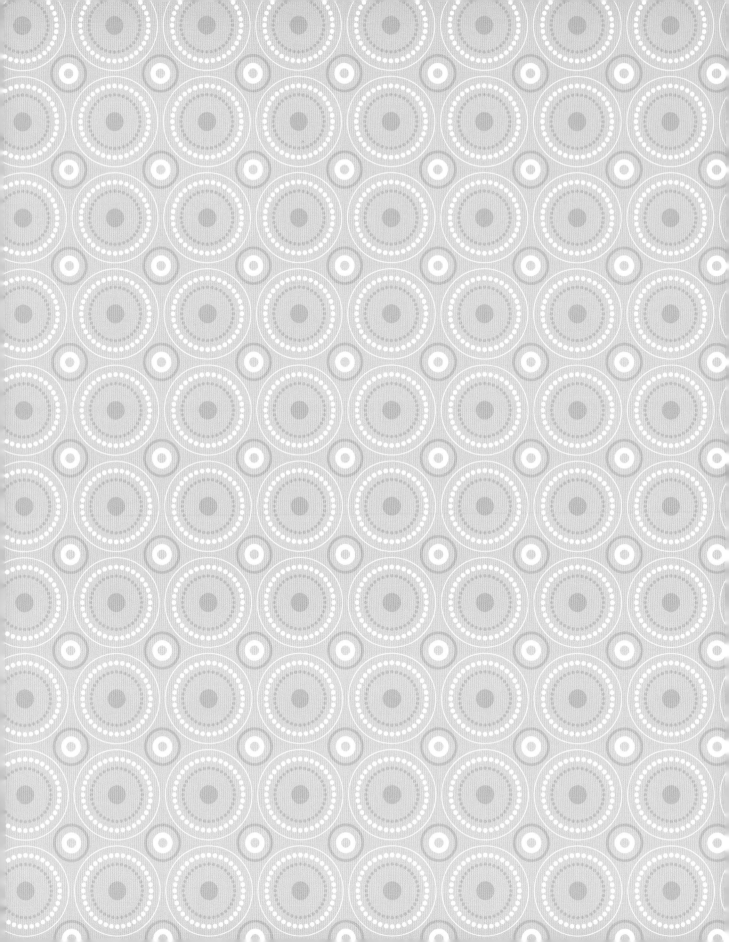

Drizzle & Dip

cook | bake | share | eat

samantha linsell

contents

introduction

It has been said that cooking cannot be taught; it has
to be caught – and for as long as I can remember I've been
fascinated with mixing ingredients together to see what
results. Luckily I had parents who nurtured this culinary
interest from an early age.

Food has always been the biggest adventure of my life;
it constantly inspires me. I cook because I love to experiment
and play with ideas. I cook because I desire certain flavours
at certain times. I cook because I love to share and connect
with people. But mostly I cook because I love to eat!

After many years of working in and around the food industry,
I took the plunge and decided to focus my life and career around
food – which led to the creation of Drizzle & Dip, my food blog.

I've written this cookbook as a continuation of this joyful
place, which is about the food I love to eat and ingredients
that excite me. It's a collection of recipes that I hope will inspire
you to explore, change and make your own. Some are
favourites from my blog and others are new.

So seasons aside, this is a collection of recipes
to be enjoyed morning, noon and night.

Enjoy!

morning

huevos rancheros

This traditional Mexican breakfast of fried eggs smothered in cooked salsa and wrapped in a warm flour tortilla is so quick and easy to make. Chipotle chillies aren't readily available in South Africa, so I substituted them with chopped pickled jalapeños and smoked dried chilli flakes. (If you do manage to find chipotle, use 2T, chopped, in adobo sauce).

Serves 4

For the salsa
1T olive oil · 1 red onion, finely chopped
1 x 410g tin chopped peeled tomatoes
½t smoked or plain chilli flakes (according to taste and heat preference)
2T chopped pickled jalapeños · ½t cumin · salt

You will also need
4 large free-range eggs · 4 flour tortillas
2 spring onions, sliced (optional) · fresh coriander leaves (optional)
1 tomato, chopped (optional)

Heat the olive oil in a pan or small pot and fry the onion until it starts to soften (about 5 minutes). Add the tinned tomatoes, chilli, jalapeños, cumin and salt and simmer gently for about 10 minutes.

While it's simmering, fry the eggs.

Heat the tortillas in the microwave for about 20 seconds or dry-fry them on each side in a large nonstick pan until they are heated through.

To assemble, spread some warm salsa over the surface of a tortilla and top with an egg. Add spring onion, coriander and tomatoes or any other ingredients of your choice.

Cook's notes Fillings that go well with *huevos rancheros* include crispy bacon, avocado and grated cheese. The leftover salsa is great as a dip with corn chips, or served over nachos.

pork sausages
with honey & rosemary

This recipe elevates the humble pork sausage to another level!
To prevent the sausages from splitting and losing their juiciness,
cook them slowly over a low heat.

Serves 4

6 – 8 good-quality pork sausages • 2T butter
2t roughly chopped fresh rosemary • 2T honey to drizzle

Fry the sausages over a low heat in half the butter, turning all the time.
When they are done, add the rest of the butter and the rosemary. The butter
turns the bangers golden brown. When they are nicely coated, drizzle over the
honey and allow the sauce to start bubbling, then remove from the
heat immediately. (If you cook them too much at this stage, the butter
and honey will turn into toffee.)

Cook's notes You could add a dash of Dijon mustard to the glaze, or simply
dip the sausages in it afterwards. I sometimes sprinkle them with toasted
sesame seeds for added crunch.

bacon & leek croissant pudding
with cheese & onion

Perfect for brunch, this savoury pudding is a great way of using up stale croissants. If you find all-butter croissants too rich, try adding soft white breads, like *challah* or *kitke* to lighten it up a bit. For a vegetarian option, leave out the bacon and add mushrooms.

Serves 6

4 stale croissants (about 400g) · 150 – 200g streaky bacon, diced
2T butter · 1 onion, finely chopped · 4 leeks (white only), finely sliced
1T chopped parsley · 1T chopped thyme
3 large free-range eggs · 1 cup cream · 1½ cups milk
1 cup grated cheese (I use half mature Cheddar and half Gruyère)
½t chilli flakes (optional) · 1t smoked paprika (optional)
a pinch grated nutmeg · salt · freshly ground black pepper

Preheat the oven to 180°C. Tear the croissants into small pieces and place in a large bowl. Fry the bacon in a nonstick pan until crispy and then set aside to drain on kitchen paper. Add the butter to the remaining bit of bacon fat and sauté the onion and leeks over a low heat until they soften (about 6 to 8 minutes). Add the bacon back into the pan, then add the parsley and thyme and remove from the heat.

In another bowl, whisk the eggs, then add the cream, milk, cheese, chilli flakes and spices. Add the bacon mix to the egg mix and pour the whole lot over the torn croissants. Mix well, allowing the liquid to soak in for a few minutes. Empty the mixture into an appropriately sized ovenproof dish and bake for an hour to 75 minutes (depending on how thick the mix is) until it turns golden brown and puffs up.

Cook's notes I loosely cover the dish with foil after 30 minutes of baking to prevent it from overbrowning. If you like your pudding crispy, use a larger baking dish and spread the mixture thinner; if you prefer it soft and moist, bake it in a deeper dish and watch it puff up like a soufflé.

baked eggs

Eggs are amazingly versatile – and this recipe gives them the X factor. You can add any ingredients or flavours to the basic recipe.

Serves 4

butter for greasing (or cooking spray) · 4 large free-range eggs
4T cream · 1T freshly chopped herbs (thyme, parsley, dill, chives)
salt · freshly ground black pepper

Optional extras
lightly steamed asparagus · baby tomatoes
grated cheese (I like Gruyère and Parmesan) · crispy bacon (pre-cooked)
blanched spinach (drained and chopped up) · lightly fried mushrooms
chilli · paprika · Tabasco

Preheat your oven to 180°C. Lightly butter or spray a gratin dish and break the eggs into it, ensuring they cover the surface of the dish. Add the cream, then nestle the optional extras of your choice into the egg and cream mixture. Season. Bake for 10 to 15 minutes, or until the eggs are done to your preference.

Cook's notes You could turn these into Mexican-style baked eggs by leaving out the cream and using a spicy tomato sauce instead. (see *huevos rancheros* on page 15).

roasted butternut, bacon & feta frittata

I cook frittatas almost every week, as they go well with a wide variety of ingredients. I often combine two or three of the following cheeses: chevin, Parmesan, Chedddar, feta and Gruyère. Ham, salami, bacon, chorizo and leftover sausages also go well. I like to freshen mine up with chopped vegetables and herbs, adding chilli, smoked paprika and cayenne pepper for extra zing. Frittatas are great for breakfast, a light lunch or supper. They also make delicious picnic food, eaten cold.

Serves 4

1 medium butternut, peeled and cut into small cubes (about 2 – 3 cups)
olive oil for drizzling · 100g bacon, chopped · 4 spring onions,
finely sliced · 8 large free-range eggs · 100ml milk or cream
100g feta, crumbled · 1T chopped thyme
salt · freshly ground black pepper

Preheat the oven to 180°C. Place the butternut on a baking tray
and drizzle with olive oil, coating lightly. Bake for 25 minutes until
soft and starting to brown around the edges. Remove from the oven
and allow to cool for about 5 minutes.

In the meantime, heat a nonstick frying pan and fry the bacon until crispy.
Add the spring onions and fry for a minute.

Beat the eggs lightly and then add the milk. Add the butternut, bacon
and spring onions to the egg mixture and then add the feta and thyme.
Pour the entire mixture into an ovenproof container, or back into the frying pan,
and bake for 20 to 25 minutes until golden brown and firm to the touch.

summer fruit salad

with mint, ginger & lime dressing

Summer is the season when juicy, plump fruit is abundant.
This fragrant and sweet dressing adds zing to what is
already naturally perfect.

a variety of summer fruit, cut according to your preference
160ml water • 6T sugar • 1T chopped mint
6cm fresh ginger, grated • juice of 1 lime (or lemon)
fresh mint, to serve (optional)

Cut a selection of your favourite fruit into different shapes,
or scoop them into balls and place in a bowl.

To make the dressing, place the water and sugar in a small pot and
bring it to the boil, allowing it to simmer for about 5 minutes until it thickens.
In a bowl mix the mint, ginger and lime juice, then pour the hot sugar-syrup
over it, muddling lightly with a wooden spoon. Allow it to cool and then strain
out the mint leaves and ginger, and place the dressing in the fridge to cool.

Drizzle it over your salad just before serving and add some fresh mint if you like.

decadent breakfast oats

Since I've started adding apples, pears, cinnamon and nuts to my morning oats, I can't go back to eating them any other way. It's an excellent way of sneaking some extra nutrition into children's meals without them noticing. A drizzle of honey or slightly fruity maple syrup adds a delicious finishing touch.

Serves 2

2 cups water · 1 cup oats (not the instant variety)
a pinch salt · 1 apple, peeled, cored and cut into thick chunks
1 pear, peeled, cored and cut into chunks · 1t cinnamon
raw nuts, for sprinkling · crushed mixed seeds (optional)
honey or maple syrup for drizzling

Bring the water to the boil and add the oats and salt. Add the chopped fruit and cinnamon. Stir the oats occasionally, adding more boiling water from the kettle if necessary. When the oats are cooked, ladle into a bowl and sprinkle over the nuts. Lastly, drizzle with honey or maple syrup.

Cook's notes So many things complement cooked oats; add any combination of these to yours: fresh banana, stewed fruit, prunes, poached apples and pears, whisky, honey, maple syrup, milk, cream, nuts, berries, dried berries, raisins, sugar, muesli and oat bran. Crushed seeds (sesame, linseed, pumpkin and sunflower) are also delicious in oats. I keep a jar in my fridge, which I sprinkle onto mine for extra crunch (and my daily dose of Omega 3 and 6 oils).

ricotta crumpets
with warm strawberry sauce

I love crumpets. If you add ricotta to the batter you'll get a much richer, fluffier and not as sweet result, which is perfect for this warm strawberry sauce. Crumpets go beautifully with honey and yoghurt, or maple syrup and cream. Fresh fruit and nuts wouldn't go amiss either.

Serves 4

3 large free-range eggs, separated · 1½ cups flour · 1½t baking powder
1 cup buttermilk · ½ cup milk · 2t vanilla extract
200g ricotta · butter for frying

For the sauce
400g (about 3 cups) strawberries (fresh or frozen)
½ cup sugar

Whisk the egg whites until they form stiff peaks and set aside.
Place all the remaining ingredients, except the ricotta and butter, into a separate bowl and lightly whisk to form a batter. Gently stir the ricotta and beaten egg whites through the batter.

Heat a nonstick frying pan and add a knob of butter.
Drop generous tablespoons of batter into the pan, turning them as the surface starts to bubble. Drain on kitchen paper.

To make the strawberry sauce, heat the strawberries and sugar in a small pot and cook for 8 to 10 minutes, stirring occasionally, until the mixture is the consistency of a chunky sauce. Allow the sauce to cool slightly and pour generously over the crumpets.

french toast

with caramelised pears & gorgonzola

This is one of my most decadent sweet breakfast treats. I love using raisin bread, *challah* or *kitke,* as the soft cake-like texture of the bread soaks up the egg beautifully.

Serves 2

3 large free-range eggs · ¼ cup milk · 1t vanilla extract
4 slices bread · 2T butter
2 pears, trimmed, cored and cut into 8 wedges lengthways
6T brown sugar · 80g Gorgonzola (or as much as you like)

Beat the eggs until fluffy, then add the milk and vanilla extract.
Soak the bread in the egg mixture, allowing it to absorb on both sides.
Heat 1T butter in a frying pan and fry a slice or 2 of bread at a time
on both sides until golden brown. Repeat with the balance of the bread,
adding butter when necessary. Remove from the pan.

Lightly fry the pears in the remaining butter in a small pot until heated through.
Sprinkle over the brown sugar and allow it to mix with the butter until it forms
a sticky caramel. Cook the pears in the caramel until some of the juices are
extracted and the pears just start to soften.

Sprinkle a few chunks of Gorgonzola over the French toast, then arrange
the pears on top. Drizzle over the caramel sauce to melt the cheese.

raisin scones

This very easy recipe makes perfect, well-risen scones in an hour.
Serve them straight out the oven with butter and jam.

Makes 14 to 16 scones

75g butter · 2 large free-range eggs + 1 for brushing
75g sugar · 4t baking powder · 230ml milk
500g cake or bread flour + extra for dusting
1 cup raisins

Put all the ingredients, except the flour and raisins, in a mixer with
a paddle attachment and mix on a low speed until combined.

Add the flour and raisins and mix briefly. Turn the dough out onto a floured
surface, knead slightly and flatten out to a thickness of about 4 to 5cm
(I use my fingers to do this).

Press out scones using a round 58mm cookie cutter and place
on a lined baking tray. Beat an egg and brush over the tops
of the scones. Chill the scones for about 30 minutes
while you preheat the oven to 200°C. Brush a second layer of egg
over the scones to give them a really nice glaze, and bake for
15 minutes until well-risen and golden brown.

rosemary & olive oil bread

with walnuts

This wonderful bread – not quite sweet or savoury –
epitomises the perfect combination of flavours.

Makes 1 loaf

oil for greasing (or cooking spray) • 2½ cups cake flour
2t baking powder • ¼t salt • ¼ cup sugar (white or brown)
½ – ¾ cup roughly chopped walnuts • 3t dried rosemary
finely grated zest of 1 large lemon or 2 small lemons
2 large free-range eggs • ½ cup extra-virgin olive oil
¾ cup apple juice

Preheat the oven to 180°C and lightly grease
a 22 x 12cm loaf pan with oil or cooking spray.

Sift the flour, baking powder and salt into a bowl,
then add the sugar, walnuts, rosemary and zest.

In a separate bowl, beat the eggs, then add the olive oil and apple juice.
Gently stir the wet ingredients into the dry until combined, then pour
into the loaf pan. Smooth the dough and bake for about 1 hour,
or until golden and a sharp knife inserted comes out clean.

banana bread
with cranberries & walnuts

The cranberries and walnuts in this recipe make an already delicious loaf even more scrumptious. It's so easy to whip up and an excellent way to use up rapidly ripening bananas. For a more traditional loaf, leave out the cranberries and nuts and add an extra banana.

Makes 1 loaf

55g softened butter · ¾ cup sugar
2 large free-range eggs · 1t vanilla extract
4 large bananas, roughly mashed (you could mash half and slice half)
½ cup chopped walnuts · ¾ cup dried cranberries
1¾ cup flour · 1½t baking powder
½t bicarbonate of soda
½t salt

Preheat the oven to 180°C and line a 22 x 12cm loaf tin with baking paper. Using an electric mixer, cream the butter and sugar until fluffy, then add the eggs, one at a time, ensuring they are thoroughly incorporated before adding the next. Add the vanilla extract, banana, walnuts and cranberries and mix briefly. Sift the dry ingredients and mix quickly to combine. Spread the batter into the loaf tin and bake for 55 minutes, or until a sharp knife inserted comes out clean.

Cook's notes If you find the top of your banana bread is darkening too quickly, cover it loosely with a piece of foil while baking. If you're using a deep tin you may need to bake the loaf for a bit longer.

10-minute strawberry jam

I've been making jam since I was a child – I really love the concept of preserving fruit and changing it into something different – but it was always a mammoth task that took the better part of a day. Since discovering this quick method of making jam in smaller batches, I don't want to do it any other way. The end result is so much more about the fruit and less about the sugar. However, it doesn't have the same shelf life as jam made the traditional way. In the fridge, it should keep for at least a month.

Makes about 500ml

500g (about 3 heaped cups) strawberries
1 cup sugar • 2T lemon juice

Place all the ingredients into a large, shallow pan and cook over a high heat for 8 to 10 minutes. The wider the base of the pan, the better – as it facilitates evaporation and quicker setting. To test if the jam is ready, place a side plate in the freezer for 5 minutes. Drop a dollop of jam onto the cold plate. Run your finger through the middle and if the jam stays apart and doesn't immediately join back together, it's jammy enough. I set a timer and find that 10 minutes usually guarantees good jam.

While you're making the jam, sterilise storage jars in a large pot of boiling water, remove and drain. Scoop the hot jam into the jars and seal. Pop the sealed jars back into the boiling water for 10 minutes (this gets rid of any bacteria). Remove from the pot, drain and allow to cool.

noon

crispy noodle slaw

This family favourite ranks as one of my all-time best salads.
I love the texture and flavour combinations of the seeds and
almonds and the peppery taste of the raw cabbage. It's great with
grilled meat and fish dishes, and makes a perfect braai partner.
A dash of wasabi added to the sweet and salty
dressing gives it a wonderful kick.

Serves 4 – 6

For the salad
half a medium cabbage, finely shredded
4 spring onions, finely sliced (the white and some of the green parts)
1 celery stalk, finely sliced
1 cup mangetout (or sugarsnap peas), finely cut lengthways
a handful toasted almond flakes
a handful toasted sunflower seeds
1 packet 2-minute noodles, broken up and toasted

For the dressing
2T soya sauce · ¼ cup red wine vinegar · ⅓ cup sunflower oil
⅓ cup honey (or syrup) · 1 garlic clove, crushed
½ – 1t wasabi paste (optional)

Cut up all the vegetables and mix in a salad bowl.

Dry-fry the seeds and almonds in a pan until light brown, then set aside.

Toast the broken-up noodles under the grill and set aside.

Pour all the dressing ingredients into an empty jar and shake. Just before
serving, soak the salad in the tangy dressing and toss well.

salad nachos

The addition of raw ingredients to one of my favourite snacks
makes it a fresher and healthier option.

Serves 2

½ cup salsa (shop-bought or a home-made 'cheat's' version *)
2 cups corn chips • ½ cup grated Cheddar or mozzarella
salad (chopped-up peppers, cucumber, cooked corn, red onions, fresh
tomatoes, avocado) • fresh coriander for sprinkling

Switch on the grill and place the rack in the middle of the oven.
Heat the chips in the microwave for a minute to make them more crunchy.
Cover the surface of a baking tray or dish with a layer of chips and
then spread over the salsa. Sprinkle with grated cheese and place under
the grill until the cheese has melted. Doing this in the middle of the
oven, rather than directly under the grill, allows the salsa and cheese
to heat up to a nice gooey consistency.

Remove from the oven and top with scattered
salad ingredients and fresh coriander.

* For the home-made 'cheat's' salsa
1 ripe tomato, chopped • ½ red onion, finely chopped • 2T jar salsa

warm potato salad
with lemon & mint

In this twist on a traditional potato salad, I've substituted some of the mayonnaise with crème fraîche, which makes it much lighter. The mint gives the dish a fresh lift, making it a perfect accompaniment to grilled fish or lamb.

Serves 4 – 6

700g new potatoes · 1 x 250g tub crème fraîche
4T good-quality mayonnaise · zest of 1 lemon
juice of ½ lemon · 2T finely chopped fresh mint
salt · freshly ground black pepper

Boil the potatoes until just done, then drain. Mix all the other ingredients together and toss through the potatoes.

Serve warm (allow the potatoes to cool slightly after boiling) or cold.

Cook's notes Another variation is to add a small bunch of chopped spring onions, and replace the mint with chives or parsley.
For a spicy version, you could replace the lemon and mint with 1T of smoky chipotle, chilli sauce or Tabasco.

pear, blue cheese & walnut salad

This salad's flavour combinations (sweet maple dressing and salty blue cheese) make it a difficult-to-beat classic. Use whichever lettuce leaves you prefer. Rocket works wonderfully, adding a peppery dimension.

Serves 4

2 generous handfuls rocket (or leaves of your choice)
2 pears, sliced · 150g blue cheese, broken into chunks
50g crushed walnuts for sprinkling

For the vinaigrette
4T olive oil · 2T red wine vinegar
4t maple syrup · ½t Dijon mustard · salt

Place the salad ingredients in a bowl, or arrange on a platter.
Mix all the vinaigrette ingredients in a small jar
and shake well before drizzling over the salad.

Cook's notes It's best to make the salad just before serving,
as the pears brown very quickly.

hummus

These three variations on a classic hummus recipe add a colour and taste boost to any starter platter. Hummus keeps in the fridge for up to a week, so it can be made in advance. I like to serve it with toasted garlic pita triangles* (made from pita bread, which I always have in my freezer).

Each recipe serves 4 – 6

Roasted butternut hummus

1 medium butternut, peeled and cut into small cubes
3T olive oil + extra for drizzling · 1 garlic clove, crushed
3T tahini · ¼ cup water · 1t ground cumin
salt · freshly ground black pepper

Preheat the oven to 200°C. Place the butternut cubes in a roasting dish and drizzle lightly with olive oil. Roast for about 20 to 30 minutes until the cubes start to caramelise around the edges. Remove from the oven and allow to cool.

Run the butternut through a food processor with the remaining ingredients until a thick, paste-like consistency develops. You can add water if it needs thinning down. Adjust the seasoning until you're happy with the flavour combinations.

* To make pita triangles
Cut a pita in half, then cut the rounds into 4 or 8 triangles. Brush with garlic olive oil and toast on either side under a grill until golden brown and crispy.

continues on page 54…

…continued from page 52

Roasted beetroot hummus

5 or 6 medium beetroots (about 450g), peeled and quartered
3T olive oil + extra for drizzling · 4T tahini
1 – 2 garlic cloves, crushed (depending on how garlicky you like it)
juice of 1 lemon · 1t ground cumin · 1t coriander
salt · freshly ground black pepper
a small handful smoked macadamia nuts or pine nuts for sprinkling

Preheat the oven to 200°C and place the beetroot in a
roasting dish and drizzle lightly with olive oil. Roast for about
30 to 40 minutes until it starts to caramelise around the edges.
Remove from the oven and allow to cool.

Run the beetroot through a food processor with the remaining
ingredients until a thick, paste-like consistency develops.
Add a splash of olive oil if you want to thin it out, and adjust the
seasoning until you're happy with the flavour combinations.
I like to sprinkle over chopped roasted macadamia or pine nuts.

Green pea hummus

500g fresh or frozen peas
3T olive oil + extra for drizzling · 3T tahini · 1½t ground cumin
1 – 3 garlic cloves (depending on how garlicky you like it)
a pinch chilli flakes (or more if you like it spicy)
a small handful mint, chopped · squeeze of lemon
salt · freshly ground pepper

Blanch the peas in boiling water for about 5 minutes, then strain in
a colander under cold water. Blend in a food processor with the other
ingredients until a smooth consistency forms. Adjust the
seasoning until you're happy with the flavour combinations.
Place in the fridge to set and drizzle over some olive oil just before serving.

green olive
salsa verde
with linguini

This recipe, featured on the cover of this book, is a twist on the Italian salsa verde – with the green olives adding a wonderful depth of flavour and meaty texture.

Serves 2

½ cup finely chopped green olives • 2T finely chopped flat-leaf parsley
1T chopped mint • 1 garlic clove, crushed
½ cup extra-virgin olive oil • zest of ½ lemon
1T lemon juice • 200g linguini
freshly grated Parmesan, to serve
freshly ground black pepper

To make the salsa verde, mix the olives, herbs, garlic, olive oil, lemon zest and lemon juice in a bowl. Let it stand for a few hours or overnight so the flavours can develop and infuse the oil.

Stir the salsa verde through freshly boiled *al dente* linguini.

Serve with freshly grated Parmesan and a crack of black pepper.

mushroom pâté
with melba toast

This pâté combines fresh mushrooms with rehydrated
dried porcini or shiitake to really concentrate the flavour.
It takes time, but is well worth the effort. Melba toast
is a healthier alternative to crackers – I always make
as many as can fit in my oven.

Serves 4

⅓ cup dried mushrooms (porcini or shiitake), rehydrated in 200ml boiling water
½ cup vegetable stock · ½ onion, finely chopped
4 garlic cloves, crushed · 2T butter
2 cups mushrooms, chopped (any or a mix)
¼ cup white wine · 4T chopped parsley
½ cup cream cheese · freshly ground black pepper

Soak the dried mushrooms in boiling water for at least 20 minutes,
then drain and place the liquid in a pot with the stock, onion and garlic.
Bring it to the boil and cook until no liquid remains (about 10 minutes).
Add the butter, rehydrated and fresh mushrooms and
cook for about 4 minutes. Add the wine and allow the liquid to
cook off. Blend the cooked mushrooms with the cream cheese
and parsley, seasoning generously with black pepper. Spoon the pâté
into serving dishes and chill until ready to serve.

To make melba toast
Stale bread makes the best melba toast – I like to use focaccia
or sourdough, sliced very finely with an electric carving knife.
Place bread slices onto a baking tray (or on a cooling rack on a
baking tray) and place in a preheated oven (around 150°C) for about
20 minutes. Turn the bread once, about halfway through.
Stored in an airtight container, the toast keeps for weeks.

chicken liver pâté

with crispy flatbreads

This is my favourite chicken liver pâté recipe, which I've been making for years. It takes only 10 minutes and is a regular feature in my picnic basket.

Serves 4

125g butter + a bit extra for coating the top
1 large onion, chopped · 250g chicken livers
1 – 2 garlic cloves, crushed · 1 bay leaf
20ml brandy · salt · freshly ground black pepper

Melt the butter in a pan and sauté the onions for a couple of minutes. Add the chicken livers, garlic and bay leaf and cook over a moderate heat, stirring until the chicken livers are just done (about 4 minutes). Add the brandy. Remove from the heat and allow to cool.

Remove the bay leaf and blend the chicken livers in a food processor, seasoning with a bit of salt and lots of black pepper. Spoon into ramekins or other serving dishes and allow to cool. When cool, melt some butter (in the microwave) to pour over the pâté, which looks pretty decorated with a bay leaf. Chill in the fridge until serving.

Cook's notes This pâté freezes well.

continues on page 61…

…continued from page 58

crispy flatbreads

This recipe was generously given to me by Kirsten Zschokke, owner of Miss K Food Café in Green Point. I like to place a platter of piled-up breads in the middle of the table so people can break off shards as they eat.

Makes 12 – 14

1kg flour · 2t salt · 10g instant yeast powder (1 packet)
2T sugar · 800ml lukewarm water · olive oil for brushing
salt and dried rosemary for sprinkling

Place the flour, salt, yeast and sugar in a mixer with the paddle attachment set to low. Add the water and mix on low for about 8 to 10 minutes. Remove the paddle and leave the dough in the mixing bowl, covered with a tea towel. Store in a warm place for 1 to 2 hours, allowing it to prove until the dough appears to rise out of the bowl.

Preheat the oven to 200°C. Punch the dough (which is still fairly sticky) back and empty it onto a well-floured surface. Break off a small ball, knead it briefly and roll it out very thinly – as thin as it will go without tearing. Then place it on a greased baking tray (or one that has been lined with baking paper or silicone sheets). Brush the dough generously with olive oil, sprinkle over the salt and rosemary and bake for about 15 minutes until golden brown. Keep watching it. Repeat until you have completed all of your flatbreads.

Cook's notes If you prefer your breads plain, leave out the rosemary and sprinkle only sea salt. Halve the recipe if you want a smaller batch.

zucchini
& prawn pizza
with cream-soaked mozzarella

Once you use buffalo mozzarella soaked in cream on your pizzas, you won't look back. The flavour combination of zucchini and prawns is sublime.

Makes 2 large pizzas

2 ready-made pizza bases (or make your own using your favourite recipe)
½ cup tomato purée
6 zucchini, thinly sliced with a potato peeler and cut into thin strips
2T olive oil + extra for drizzling · juice of ½ lemon
salt · freshly ground black pepper
12 – 16 prawns · 1 garlic clove, crushed
1 green chilli, finely chopped
250 – 350g buffalo mozzarella ball
125ml cream for soaking the ball (at least an hour before use or overnight)
fresh basil or thyme, to garnish

Preheat the oven to 200°C (for the ready-made pizza bases). Spread a thin layer of purée on each pizza. Place the zucchini ribbons in a bowl and toss with 1T of olive oil and half the lemon juice, salt and pepper.

In another bowl, mix the prawns with the garlic, chilli, 1T of olive oil, and the balance of the lemon juice. In a preheated pan, fry the prawns very quickly in the sauce until they start to change colour but are not cooked through.

Break the pre-soaked mozzarella into chunks and arrange on top of the pizza with the 'ribbons' and the chilli-and-garlic-basted prawns and bake for 8 to 10 minutes until the crust turns golden and the mozzarella has melted.

When it comes out the oven, drizzle with olive oil and scatter with fresh basil or a few sprigs of thyme.

Cook's notes Not a seafood fan? Use bacon or prosciutto instead of prawns. Refrigerate the leftover cream for use in other dishes.

caramelised onion & mushroom pies

A sprinkle of sesame seeds gives these comforting vegetarian pastries added crunch.

Serves 4

For the filling
50g butter · 3 red onions, finely sliced
500g mushrooms, sliced (brown or a mix) · 2T balsamic vinegar
1T chopped thyme · 1T brown sugar · salt · freshly ground black pepper

1 large, free-range egg, beaten
(for brushing over the edges and tops of the pies)
sesame seeds for sprinkling (optional)

Melt the butter in a frying pan and sauté the onions until they start to soften (about 5 minutes). Add the mushrooms and cook for a further 5 minutes. Add the rest of the ingredients and cook until the liquid has evaporated and it is the consistency of a sticky relish. Season with salt and pepper. Set aside to cool while you make the pastry.

For the pastry recipe turn to page 141.

Roll out the dough on a floured surface and cut into rectangular shapes. You will need two rectangles for each pie. Divide the filling evenly among the pie bases, leaving enough dough around the edges for sealing, then brush these with egg. Cut slits in the pastry lid and place on top of the base, pressing down around the edges. Brush the whole pie with egg and sprinkle with sesame seeds. Place the pies in the fridge while you preheat the oven to 200°C. Bake for 30 to 35 minutes until golden brown.

Cook's notes I use a chilled bottle of water or wine to roll the pastry, which keeps it as cool as possible. If you want to bypass making the pastry, buy ready-made butter puff pastry and roll it out so that it's even thinner.

pork sausage rolls
with apple, sage & cider

Home-made sausage rolls are infinitely better than
shop-bought ones. These are guaranteed to be gobbled
up by your guests as they come out of the oven.

Serves 4 – 6

1T butter · 1 onion, finely chopped · 1 apple, grated
½ cup cider · 500g pork mince
1 cup breadcrumbs · 2T finely chopped sage
2T finely chopped parsley · salt · white pepper
1 roll ready-made puff pastry, thawed
1 large free-range egg, beaten

Preheat the oven to 200°C. Heat the butter in a nonstick frying pan
and fry the onion for a few minutes until just softened. Add the apple
and fry for a further 2 minutes. Add the cider and allow the liquid to cook off.

In a bowl, mix the mince with the onion-and-apple mixture,
breadcrumbs and herbs and season very generously with salt
and pepper (white pepper goes so well with pork).

Roll out the puff pastry onto a floured surface and, if necessary,
roll it further until it is about 3mm thick. Cut the pastry in half and place
enough mixture down the middle to make a sausage thick enough to
roll over – the pastry should overlap slightly when you join the two
sides. Brush the joined edge with egg, then turn the roll so that the join
is on the underside. Cut to the desired length, then brush the tops of
each roll with egg and bake for 20 minutes until they are golden brown.

lamb burger
with zucchini tzatziki

These juicy, flavour-packed lamb burgers can
be made with beef mince, if you prefer.

Serves 4 – 6

4T olive oil for frying · 1 small onion, finely chopped
2 garlic cloves, crushed · 500g lamb mince
1T finely chopped parsley (preferably Italian flat-leaf)
1T finely chopped fresh mint · 1T oregano (dried or fresh)
1t ground cumin · ½t ground coriander · ½ cup breadcrumbs
1 large free-range egg · ¼ cup tomato sauce
1t dried chilli flakes (optional, for extra heat) · salt
freshly ground black pepper · 4 burger buns, toasted on each side
lettuce, sliced tomato and sliced red onion, to serve

For the zucchini tzatziki
4 medium zucchini, grated · 1 cup plain yoghurt
1 garlic clove, crushed · 1t dried oregano · 1t chopped fresh mint
juice of ¼ lemon · olive oil · salt · freshly ground black pepper

Heat 1T of olive oil in a nonstick frying pan and sauté the onion
and garlic briefly until they start to soften. In a bowl, mix the mince
with the onion-and-garlic mix and add the rest of the ingredients and
mix well. Season generously with salt and pepper.

Divide the mince into even parts and roll into balls, which you will
then press down to make patties. Heat 1T of olive oil in a pan. Fry the
first batch of patties and, if necessary, wipe the pan with a paper towel
between batches in case any burnt bits are left behind.

Place the grated zucchini on a clean kitchen towel or muslin and wring several
times until all the liquid has been squeezed out. When drained, place
it in a bowl with all the other ingredients and mix. Season to taste.

To serve, place the patty on a toasted bun, and top it with a generous
spoon of tzatziki. Add lettuce, fresh tomato and onion if you like.

Cook's notes The lamb mince should not be too lean,
otherwise the patties will be too dry.

pork burger
with apple & red onion slaw

I love the flavour of bacon in this burger recipe.
The green apple slaw complements the pork beautifully.

Makes 4 large burgers

For the burgers
oil for frying · 100g (about 6 – 7 slices) streaky bacon, finely chopped
1 small onion, finely chopped · 1 garlic clove, crushed
450 – 500g pork mince · 2t finely chopped sage
1T chopped parsley · salt · freshly ground black pepper
4 burger buns, toasted on each side

For the slaw
1 cup finely shredded cabbage · 1 cup grated or finely cut carrots
½ cup green apples cut into matchstick-size strips
½ cup thinly sliced red onion · ¼ cup mayonnaise
a splash of Tabasco (or any hot sauce, according to your heat preference)

Fry the bacon and onion in a pan until the onions have softened
(about 5 minutes). Add the garlic and cook for a further minute or so.

In a bowl, combine the pork, bacon mix and herbs. Mould the
mixture into 4 large burgers or 6 smaller ones.

To make the slaw, combine all the ingredients in a bowl.

Heat a griddle pan and cook the burgers for about 5 minutes on
either side until cooked through. You could also cook these on a braai.

Stuff a toasted bun with a juicy burger and a fresh helping of slaw.

Cook's notes Feeling decadent? Stuff chunks of cheese into the
middle of each patty before cooking.

slow-roasted ginger beer pulled pork bánh mì

with pickled carrot & daikon

If you have never tried making pulled pork, I urge you to try it. It's time-consuming, but requires little effort and yields juicy, succulent roast pork that's great for sandwiches. You'll need a pork leg or shoulder – Boston butt is preferable, but either cut will do. Don't go bigger than 3kg, as you want as much of the flavour to permeate the meat as possible. I love it served on a baguette, Vietnamese bánh mì style, with pickled vegetables.

Serves 10 – 14

2 onions, peeled and quartered · 1 pork leg (approximately 3kg)
1 litre ginger beer · ¼ cup brown sugar
sliced cucumber, fresh coriander and baguettes, to serve

For the pork rub
½ cup brown sugar · 4 garlic cloves, crushed
10cm fresh ginger, grated · 1t dried ginger
1T smoked paprika · 2T sea salt or kosher salt
1 – 2t chilli powder (depending how spicy you like it)
1T sesame oil

For the pickled vegetables
2 cups warm water · 2T rice vinegar
3T sugar · 4T salt · 3 carrots, sliced julienne
1 small daikon, peeled and sliced julienne

continues on page 75…

...continued from page 72

Mix the rub ingredients in a large bowl,
then coat the pork with it, ensuring it's completely covered.
Place into a Ziploc bag and chill in the fridge overnight.

Preheat the oven to 170°C. Place the onions in a deep roasting pan.
If you like crispy crackling, remove the thick fat layer from the leg and cook
it separately as the slow-cooking process will soften it. Otherwise, leave
it on and remove it at the end. Place the pork on top of the onions.
Pour the ginger beer into the pan so that the pork is half-submerged.
Add the sugar. Roast for seven hours, or until the meat is very tender.
Place a piece of tinfoil loosely over the meat to prevent the top from burning.

When the pork is cooked, you will notice the sauce has reduced
and thickened. Don't be concerned if there is still quite a bit of liquid.
Using a fork, pull the meat off the bone in long strands and mix it with the pan
juices. It will soak them up like a sponge and add a lovely flavour to the meat.

To make the pickled vegetables, mix the water, vinegar, sugar and salt
and allow to cool. Place the vegetables into a clean jar and pour over the
brine solution. Allow to pickle overnight or for a few days.

Cut the baguettes, fill them with warm pulled pork and top with pickled carrot,
daikon and freshly sliced cucumber. Scatter over fresh coriander.

bang bang chicken wraps

This wonderful recipe combines chicken and crunchy greens with a spicy peanut satay sauce, all wrapped in a flour tortilla. Set the ingredients out and let everyone make their own.

Serves 4 – 6

4 chicken breasts
¼ cup ready-made barbecue basting sauce or any other suitable marinade
2T olive oil • 1 – 2 flour tortillas per person
½ cup fresh sliced cucumber • ½ cup mung bean sprouts
½ cup sliced lettuce • ½ cup sliced spring onions
fresh coriander, to serve

For the satay sauce
100g smooth or crunchy peanut butter • 3t sweet chilli sauce
1T oil (I use sesame oil, as I love its flavour)
1T water • 1t soya sauce
1T Japanese rice vinegar (optional)

To make the satay sauce, combine all the ingredients in a small pot and heat until softened and well combined. If you like it spicier, add more sweet chilli, or if you want it saltier, add more soya sauce.

To make the chicken, flatten it out or cut it into thin strips. Place in a plastic bag and coat generously with the barbecue sauce.

Heat the olive oil in a nonstick frying pan and fry the chicken until golden on both sides and cooked through. Heat the tortillas in the microwave or dry-fry in a nonstick pan.

To assemble, spread some peanut sauce on a tortilla, add the chicken, vegetables and a sprinking of coriander and wrap.

beer-battered
fish tacos
with spicy slaw

This is one of my favourite Mexican dishes and is packed with flavour. Make the pickled red onion about 4 hours in advance.

Serves 4 – 6

oil for frying · 450 – 500g firm white fish fillets, cut into strips or chunks
1¾ cups flour · 2t smoked paprika (optional)
salt · freshly ground black pepper · 3t baking powder
300ml beer · soft flour tacos or tortillas (1 – 2 per person)
1 red onion, finely sliced and soaked in red wine vinegar for 4 hours
(made in advance)
fresh coriander leaves and lime or lemon wedges, to serve

For the spicy slaw
2 cups grated carrot · 2 cups finely sliced cabbage
¼ cup good-quality mayonnaise (enough to coat the vegetables)
hot sauce (I use a Mexican chipotle hot sauce but any other chilli sauce or
chopped pickled jalapeño will work)

Heat the oil in a deep saucepan. Toss the fish with ¼ cup flour, paprika (if using) and seasoning. In another bowl, mix the remaining flour and baking powder. Add the beer and whisk lightly to form a thick batter. When the oil is hot, dip each piece of floured fish into the batter and gently drop it into the oil. Cook until golden brown on all sides, then remove from the oil and drain on kitchen paper. Repeat until all the fish is cooked.

To make the spicy slaw, toss the ingredients together and mix well.

Heat the tacos or tortillas by microwaving for 10 seconds
or dry-fry them in a hot pan.

To assemble, place a few chunks of fish in a taco or tortilla, top with slaw, pickled red onion and coriander. Season with salt and a spritz of lime juice.

lemony fish cakes

This classic recipe is a perennial crowd-pleaser. Use whatever sustainable white fish is available from your supermarket or fishmonger. Frozen fish works well, too. Serve with lemon wedges and a lovely green salad or chips.

Serves 4

350g potatoes or new potatoes · 500g sustainable white fish
6 spring onions, finely sliced
2T capers, chopped · 2T parsley, finely chopped
6 – 8 anchovy fillets, chopped (optional)
zest of 1 small lemon · 3T lemon juice (about ½ lemon)
flour for dusting · sunflower oil for frying

Bring a pot of water to the boil and add the potatoes. Place a colander or sieve over the water and add the fish. Cook with the lid on until the fish becomes flaky (about 10 minutes). Remove the fish. Continue boiling the potatoes until they are tender, then drain and mash lightly. Add the fish and all the other ingredients, except the flour and oil, and mix gently. Chill the mixture in the fridge for at least an hour – this will prevent the fish cakes from falling apart when you fry them.

Using your hands, mould the mixture into fish cakes, flatten slightly and lightly dust with flour. Heat enough oil to cover the base of a nonstick frying pan and fry the fish cakes until golden brown on both sides. Drain on kitchen paper before serving.

Cook's notes The mixture can be made in advance and chilled until ready to fry. For an Asian slant, add chilli, replace the parsley with coriander and use lime juice instead of lemon juice.

spinach & feta pies

This is my recipe for a traditional Greek spanakopita – with a little extra lemon to freshen it up.

Makes 8 – 10 medium pies

1 onion, finely chopped • olive oil for frying and brushing
400g spinach or baby spinach • 3 – 4 spring onions, finely sliced
1T chopped dill • 1T chopped parsley
a pinch freshly grated nutmeg (about ¼t)
juice of ¼ lemon • zest of ¼ lemon
120g feta cheese, crumbled • salt
freshly ground black pepper • 6 sheets phyllo pastry

Preheat the oven to 180°C. Sauté the onions in a splash of olive oil until soft (about 5 minutes). Meanwhile, bring a pot of water to the boil. Add the spinach and cook until wilted (about 3 minutes), then drain in a colander. Squeeze out any excess water and chop the spinach. Add the chopped spinach to the onion mixture and stir. Add the spring onions, herbs, nutmeg, lemon juice and zest and cook until the liquid has evaporated. Add the feta, mix and remove from the heat. Season.

Gently remove two sheets of pastry from the packaging – cover the remaining pastry with a clean, damp tea towel to prevent it from drying out. Separate the pastry sheets and brush one with olive oil, then place the unbrushed sheet on top. Brush this with olive oil too.

Cut the pastry sheets vertically into three equal pieces or, if you want to make small pies, four or five pieces. Place a dollop of spinach mixture at the bottom end of each piece of pastry and fold over to form a triangle. Continue to fold the parcel over as you work your way up the strip of pastry, maintaining the triangle shape. Repeat with the other sheets of pastry.

Place the pies on a lined baking sheet, brush with olive oil and bake for 25 to 30 minutes, or until golden brown.

slow-roasted tomato tart

with caramelised onion & gruyère

I love slow-roasted tomatoes, the flavour intensifies so
dramatically that it's really worthwhile doing them this way.
I always make extra to blend into a robust pasta sauce
or to add to a soup or salad. This recipe also works well
for individual tarts – a perfect dinner-party starter.

Serves 6 – 8

6 – 7 small tomatoes · olive oil for drizzling · a few sprigs thyme
sea salt · 200g flour · 100g butter + extra for frying
50g Parmesan cheese, finely grated · 1 large free-range egg
2 red onions, thinly sliced · 1T balsamic vinegar
1T brown sugar · 1T Dijon mustard · 80g Gruyère cheese, grated

Preheat the oven to 150°C. Cut the tomatoes in half, drizzle with
olive oil and sprinkle generously with thyme and sea salt.
Roast for 1½ hours, or until tender and caramelised.

Mix the flour and butter in a food processor until it resembles breadcrumbs.
Stir in the Parmesan and the egg and bring together to make a dough.
Wrap in clingfilm and chill in the fridge for 20 minutes.

Increase the oven temperature to 180°C. Roll out the pastry and place in a
23cm shallow tart tin. Prick the base with a fork and bake blind for 10 minutes
(I use baking paper and dried beans to cover the base). Remove the baking
paper and beans and bake for a further 5 minutes. Allow to cool slightly.

While the pastry is baking, melt a knob of butter in a frying pan
and gently fry the onion until soft (about 5 minutes). Add the balsamic
vinegar and sugar and cook for a few more minutes until the onions start
to caramelise. When the tart shell has cooled slightly, smear the base evenly
with Dijon mustard, then spread the caramelised onion over the mustard.
Sprinkle over ⅔ of the Gruyère, then top with the roast tomatoes, cut-side up.
Scatter the remaining cheese over the tarts and bake for 20 minutes.

granadilla sorbet

This is the perfect summer dessert, reminiscent of those sticky granadilla lollies we used to enjoy at the beach as children.

Makes about 1 litre

1 cup fresh orange juice
1 cup sugar
2 cups fresh granadilla pulp
2 large free-range egg whites, beaten

Place the orange juice and sugar in a saucepan over a medium heat and stir until the sugar has dissolved. Add the granadilla pulp and allow the mixture to cool before placing it in the freezer for an hour. Remove from the freezer and fold through the egg whites. Return to the freezer for an hour, then remove and scrape the sorbet. Repeat every hour until the mixture has formed ice crystals. Leave in the freezer until ready to serve.

Alternatively, pour the fruit-and-sugar mixture into an ice-cream machine and churn until the liquid takes on the texture of soft sorbet. Add the egg whites and churn for about 20 seconds to ensure that they are incorporated. Freeze until ready to serve.

my grandmother's crunchies

My paternal grandmother Betty Linsell was a legendary
cook and I have many happy memories of meals at my
grandparents' Johannesburg home. The recipe for these delicious
crunchies has been enjoyed by four generations of Linsells.

Makes approximately 16

1 cup flour · 2 cups oats
1 cup desiccated coconut · 230g butter
1T golden syrup · 1 cup brown sugar
1t bicarbonate of soda

Preheat the oven to 180°C. Mix the flour, oats and coconut in a bowl.
Melt the butter in a small saucepan, add the syrup and sugar and heat.
When the butter is bubbling, add the bicarbonate of soda, stir through
and remove from the heat. Pour the butter mixture into the dry ingredients
and mix. Using the back of a metal spoon, press the mixture into a greased
or lined baking tray (approximately 30cm x 20cm, depending on how thick
you like your crunchies). Bake for 15 minutes, then reduce the heat to
160°C and bake for a further 10 minutes, or until golden brown, making
sure they don't burn. Allow to cool in the pan before slicing.

Cook's notes If you like your crunchies crispy,
use a wider tray and spread the mixture a bit thinner.
If you prefer them chewier, use a smaller tray, so they are thicker.

white chocolate-chip cookies

with cranberries & macadamia nuts

I find American cookies completely irresistible,
especially this recipe!

Makes 16 – 20

300g white chocolate, roughly cut into chunks
100g butter · 1 large free-range egg
50g brown sugar · 85g caster sugar
1t vanilla extract · 180g (1¼ cups) flour
1t baking powder · 50g dried cranberries
50g macadamia nuts, chopped

Preheat the oven to 180°C. Melt 85g of chocolate in a double-boiler,
then allow it to cool slightly. Using an electric beater, beat the butter, egg,
brown and caster sugar and vanilla until creamy, then beat in the melted
chocolate. Stir in the flour, baking powder, cranberries, nuts and remaining
chocolate to make a stiff dough.

Using a tablespoon measure, place small mounds of dough onto
a baking tray lined with baking paper or a silicone mat, leaving a small
space between each cookie. Bake for 12 minutes, or until just turning
golden brown. Allow the cookies to cool for a few minutes, then transfer
to a wire rack to prevent them from overbrowning on the tray.

pineapple & banana cake
with cream cheese frosting

This is a very decadent cake that's moist and moreish. To turn this into a carrot cake, replace the pineapple with grated carrot, and the banana with grated apple.

Serves 12

4 large free-range eggs · 1½ cups white or brown sugar
1 cup sunflower oil · 2 cups cake flour
½t salt · 2t baking powder · 1t bicarbonate of soda
1t cinnamon · ¼t ground cloves · ¼t nutmeg
2 cups finely chopped fresh or tinned pineapple
1½ cups roughly mashed banana (about 4 small to medium bananas)
¾ cup chopped walnuts and almonds (I use mainly walnuts)

For the frosting
100g butter (room temperature) · 125g cream cheese
3 cups icing sugar · 2t lemon juice
a small handful chopped nuts, to decorate

Preheat the oven to 180°C. Grease two 22cm round cake tins, or one large ring tin. Using an electric mixer, beat the eggs and sugar until light and fluffy (about 4 minutes). Add the oil and continue beating. Sift the flour, salt, baking powder and bicarbonate of soda into the mixture and mix briefly to incorporate. Fold in the spices, fruit and nuts by hand and pour the mixture into the cake tins. Bake for an hour until firm and a skewer inserted comes out clean.

If the top of the cake is getting too dark but it is not yet baked through, loosely cover it with a piece of tinfoil. Allow the cake to cool on a wire rack before removing it from the tin.

To make the frosting, use an electric mixer to beat all the ingredients until light and fluffy. Ice the cooled cake and decorate with chopped nuts.

peanut butter shortbread

This is a twist on a classic shortbread recipe.

Makes 12 – 16 pieces

200g butter
50g crunchy or smooth peanut butter
125g caster sugar + extra for dusting
250g plain flour, sifted
125g cornflour

Preheat the oven to 150°C. Grease or line a 20 to 24cm square cake tin with baking paper. Cream the butter, peanut butter and sugar until pale and fluffy. Add the flour and cornflour and mix lightly with a spatula or wooden spoon. Using your hands, gently knead on a clean, lightly floured surface until you have a smooth dough. Press the dough into the cake tin with the back of a metal spoon and smooth the surface. Prick the dough all over with a fork and bake for 45 to 50 minutes, or until golden in colour. Dust with caster sugar while still warm. Allow to cool slightly and then cut into squares of the desired size using a sharp knife.

night

apricots stuffed with goat's cheese

& wrapped in bacon

These flavour-filled bites are fantastic served warm or cold with drinks. Or, place a handful on some lettuce leaves for an unusual salad.

Serves 6

18 soft dried Turkish apricots
90 – 180g goat's cheese (1 – 2t per apricot,
depending on how cheesy you like them)
18 streaky bacon rashers (1 per apricot)

Preheat the oven to 200°C. Cut into the middle of each apricot with a sharp knife and, using your finger, create a hollow cavity. Fill each apricot with 1 to 2t of goat's cheese. Wrap each stuffed apricot in a piece of streaky bacon, making sure to cover all the flesh of the fruit. You could stab a cocktail stick through each one if you are going to serve them at a party. Place the stuffed apricots on a baking tray and bake for 8 to 10 minutes until the bacon is crispy and the cheese starts to ooze out.

creamy onion marmalade dip

This recipe is an excellent way to transform onion marmalade into a delicious dip, but is only worthwhile if you're making big quantities, as the onions shrink down considerably during the cooking process.

Serves 8

For the onion marmalade (makes 2 cups)
4 – 5 big onions, finely sliced • 3T olive oil
½ cup red wine • salt • freshly ground black pepper
½ cup brown sugar • ¼ cup red wine vinegar
3 bay leaves (optional)

For the the dip
½ cup onion marmalade • 1 x 250g tub crème fraîche
1 x 250g tub cream cheese

In a large nonstick frying pan or a very big pot, gently fry the onions in olive oil for about 10 to 15 minutes until they soften and start to caramelise. Add the red wine and allow all the liquid to cook off (about 5 minutes). Season with a generous amount of salt and pepper, and then add sugar, vinegar and the bay leaves. Simmer with the lid on for about 20 minutes, stirring occasionally. (If your frying pan doesn't have a lid, use a baking tray to cover it.) Remove the lid and cook for a further 5 minutes. Allow to cool, fill a jar with the marmalade and store in the fridge for future use.

To make the dip, blend the marmalade, crème fraîche and cream cheese in a food processor until smooth. The dip shouldn't require any seasoning, as the onions are packed with flavour.

Serve with crisps, melba toast or crackers.

roasted aubergine
wedges
with hummus

This method of roasting aubergines uses less oil than frying, and you don't need to salt or rinse them first.

Serves 4

For the wedges
olive oil for brushing and coating · 2 aubergines, cut into 8 wedges
sea salt · ¼ cup pomegranate seeds, to garnish (optional)

For the hummus
1 x 400g tin chickpeas, drained
1 – 2 garlic cloves (depending on how potent you want it)
2T tahini · 1t ground cumin · juice of ½ lemon
a pinch salt · freshly ground black pepper
4T olive oil (or water for a low-fat version)

Preheat the oven to 180°C and brush a baking tray with olive oil. Place the wedges on the baking tray, skin-side down and brush them lightly with olive oil and bake for 40 minutes. Turn them on their side after 20 minutes, and then onto their other side again for the last 10 minutes of roasting. Remove from the oven and season to taste.

To make the hummus, blend all the ingredients together in a food processor until a smooth consistency forms. Add olive oil (or water) if it needs thinning down.

roasted aubergine & zucchini crumble

This hearty savoury crumble is ideal as a vegetarian main dish and also makes an excellent side.

Serves 4 – 6

For the filling
1 medium aubergine, cut into cubes (about 2 cups)
3 medium zucchini, sliced diagonally (about 2 cups)
2T olive oil for drizzling
3 large tomatoes, skinned and roughly chopped
3 garlic cloves, crushed · 1t chopped thyme
1t chopped parsley · salt · freshly ground black pepper

For the topping
1 cup flour · 70g butter
50g grated Gruyère or Parmesan
2t chopped fresh thyme
4t water (optional, if it's too dry)

Preheat the oven to 180°C. Grease a 28 – 30cm pie dish or any other suitably sized oven tray. I like to use a wide top so that the crumble is spread out thinly, making it nice and crunchy (or you could make it in individual ramekins). Place the aubergine and zucchini on a baking tray, drizzle with olive oil and roast for 15 minutes. While it is roasting, skin and chop the tomatoes.

To make the topping, mix the flour and butter with your fingers, then add the cheese and herbs and mix lightly until a crumble forms. If it's too dry, add a few teaspoons of water.

In a bowl, mix the tomatoes with the garlic and herbs, seasoning to taste, and add the roasted vegetables when they come out the oven. Empty the vegetable mix into the pie dish, sprinkle it with the crumble and bake in the oven for 45 minutes until it's bubbling and brown.

grilled vegetables
with lemon & olive oil

Grilling seasonal vegetables yields a tasty and
visually appealing mix, which can also be used
to fill sandwiches or as bruschetta toppings.

Serves 4

1 aubergine · 2 large zucchini
2 carrots · 150g fresh asparagus
juice of 1 lemon · olive oil for brushing and drizzling
sea salt · freshly ground black pepper

Thinly slice the vegetables (except the asparagus, which get cooked whole)
with a knife or potato peeler and brush very lightly with a bit of olive oil
on one side. Heat a griddle pan to smoking hot and cook the vegetables,
oiled-side down, in stages until they start to darken on one side. Brush
the other side with olive oil and repeat. It's not necessary to oil the carrots
on the other side, as they start to caramelise and leak juice when they cook.

Arrange the cooked vegetables on a platter and pour over the lemon juice.
Drizzle with olive oil and season generously with sea salt and pepper.

Cook's notes For extra flavour, garnish with chopped herbs
(parsley, thyme and chives) or use a herb-infused olive oil for drizzling.

creamy calamari & basil soup

with garlic toasts

This delicious soup is inspired by a friend and former restaurateur. It's best made in advance. I allow the tomato sauce to cook for a long time, allowing the flavours to intensify. It's a guaranteed hit at your next dinner party, served with flavour-packed garlic toast.

Serves 4 – 6

For the soup

3T olive oil · 1 large onion, finely chopped · 1 celery stalk, finely chopped
2 garlic cloves, crushed · ¼ cup white wine
2 x 410g tins chopped peeled tomatoes, puréed through a blender
½t dried chilli flakes · 1T brown sugar · 1t dried oregano · salt
freshly ground black pepper · 450g calamari (rings or strips, cut into cubes)
3 cups chicken stock · 2T finely chopped fresh basil · 80ml fresh cream

For the garlic toast

1 – 2 garlic cloves, crushed · salt · freshly ground black pepper
2T olive oil · a pinch dried mixed herbs · Italian bread, sliced

Heat the olive oil in a heavy-based pot, then add the onion and celery and cook until soft (about 5 minutes). Add the garlic and white wine and cook until most of the liquid has evaporated. Add the puréed tomato, chilli, sugar, oregano, salt and pepper and bring to the boil, then reduce the heat and simmer gently for about 45 minutes to an hour, stirring occasionally. Add the calamari (can be frozen) and the hot stock and cook for about 10 minutes. Then add the basil and cream and cook gently for a further 5 minutes. Check seasoning.

For the garlic toast, mix all the ingredients (except the bread) in a bowl to create a garlic-and-herb-infused oil. Brush the oil over slices of Italian bread that you have placed on an oven tray and grill in the oven until golden brown on either side.

Cook's notes You could turn this soup into a hearty seafood stew by reducing the amount of stock (from 3 cups to 2 cups) and adding chunks of fresh white fish, prawns and mussels in their shells.

steamed mussels

with white wine, garlic & thyme

These delicious mussels are ridiculously easy to make.
Soaking up the juices with your favourite bread afterwards
is the best part of the meal!

Serves 2

1 cup dry white wine
450 – 500g mussels
2 garlic cloves, crushed
4T butter · 1t chopped parsley
1T chopped thyme · crusty bread, to serve

Pour the wine into a large pot and bring it to the boil.
Add the mussels and garlic and cover the pot, allowing it to steam
for a few minutes until the shells open. Remove the lid and add the
butter and herbs and let the sauce reduce and thicken a little.

Tip into a large bowl and pour over the sauce.
Serve with fresh crusty bread.

pan-fried calamari
with bacon, red pepper, lemon & thyme

This recipe is inspired by my friend Laurence Woodburn, who taught me how to make it, and is one of my favourites on my blog. It makes a lovely starter, or tapa, served with crusty bread to soak up all the sauce.

Serves 2

500g baby calamari (tubes and tentacles)
125g good-quality dry cured bacon or prosciutto, finely chopped
1 small red pepper, finely chopped
1 small chilli, finely chopped
olive oil for frying
2 garlic cloves, crushed
juice of 1 lemon • 1T chopped parsley
1t chopped thyme • 1T butter

Slice the calamari tubes so they open into one flat piece,
and lightly score the inside flesh in a crisscross pattern.
Fry the bacon, red pepper and chilli in olive oil until
the bacon becomes crispy, then set aside.

Using the same pan, fry the calamari tentacles and tubes
in batches until they are cooked and start curling.
This only takes a couple of minutes each time.

Toss everything back in the pan and add the garlic,
lemon juice, herbs and butter and cook for a few minutes,
allowing the juice to thicken a little and the flavours to integrate.

tequila bolognese
with linguini

The tequila gives the Bolognese sauce a lovely deep flavour.
Cooked slowly over a low heat, it's the perfect winter dinner.

Serves 4

olive oil for frying · 4 rashers streaky bacon, finely chopped
1 onion, finely chopped · 1 carrot, peeled and grated
1 celery stalk, finely chopped (or small fennel bulb)
500g lean beef mince · ¼ cup good-quality tequila
3T tomato paste · 2 garlic cloves, crushed
1T finely chopped parsley · 1T finely chopped sage
1 x 410g tin chopped peeled tomatoes · 1 cup beef stock
salt · freshly ground black pepper
2T balsamic reduction (optional)
400g long-noodle pasta (such as linguini, spaghetti or tagliatelle)
grated Parmesan, to serve

Heat a splash of olive oil in a large, heavy-based pot and fry the
bacon with the onion, carrot and celery until soft (about 8 minutes).
Add the mince and cook for a few more minutes until most of the liquid
has evaporated. Add half the tequila and cook briefly. Add the tomato
paste, garlic and herbs and stir. Add the tinned tomatoes, the rest
of the tequila and the beef stock and season well with salt and pepper.
Simmer on a low heat for about 2 hours. If you're using balsamic
reduction, stir it in right at the end, then check seasoning.

Serve with *al dente* pasta and freshly grated Parmesan.

lamb-shank ragout
with pasta shells & gremolata crumb

I adore lamb shanks but find them cumbersome to eat.
With this recipe, the meat is braised slowly in red wine and tomato
sauce until it literally falls off the bone. I serve it with pasta shells,
but any pasta works. The gremolata crumb adds freshness,
flavour and crunch. Serve with crusty bread to soak up the juices.

Serves 4 – 6

olive oil for browning the meat
3 lamb shanks (about 1.5kgs)
2 celery stalks, finely chopped · 2 carrots, grated
1 onion, finely chopped
2 rashers bacon, chopped
2 – 3 garlic cloves, crushed
1 cup red wine
1 x 410g tin whole peeled tomatoes
1T chopped parsley · 1T chopped thyme
1T chopped rosemary + 1 stalk with leaves
500ml lamb stock
salt · freshly ground black pepper
1 x 500g packet of pasta
grated Parmesan, to serve (optional)
crusty bread, to serve

For the gremolata crumb
¼ cup fresh toasted breadcrumbs
1 garlic clove, crushed
2T chopped parsley
zest of ½ lemon, grated

continues on page 121…

…continued from page 118

Heat a splash of olive oil in a large pot and brown the lamb shanks
on all sides until the meat starts to caramelise and go brown. Set aside.

In the same pan add another splash of olive oil and cook all
the vegetables until they soften (about 6 minutes).
Add the bacon and garlic and cook for a further 2 minutes or so.
Add the wine and allow the liquid to reduce by half.
Add the tomatoes and all the herbs.

Put the lamb shanks back in the pot and cover with the stock.
Bring to the boil, then reduce to a low heat and allow to cook for
about 6 to 7 hours, until the meat falls off the bone. Remove the bones
and the rosemary stalk and shred the meat into the sauce.
Check seasoning and add a generous sprinkling
of salt and freshly ground black pepper.

To make the gremolata, blend all the ingredients
in a food processor and set aside until ready to serve.

To serve, spoon some of the meaty sauce over a plate of
al dente pasta and sprinkle with grated Parmesan and
gremolata crumb. Place a platter of crusty bread in the middle
of the table for soaking up the sauce.

roasted vegetable lasagne

with aubergine, mushroom & peppers

Chef and restaurateur Jane Touwen inspired this recipe.
She taught it to some friends on one of her courses many years
ago and they passed it on to me. It's fairly time-consuming, as
there are a few separate components to prepare, but well worth it.

Serves 6

For the tomato sauce
1 large red onion, finely chopped
2 garlic cloves, crushed
2T olive oil
2 x 410g tins chopped peeled tomatoes
¼ cup white wine • 1t sugar
salt • freshly ground black pepper

For the lasagne
250g mushrooms, sliced
1T olive oil + extra for brushing
2 large aubergine (about 600g) • 3 red or yellow peppers
½ cup basil leaves, shredded
lasagne sheets to make 2 layers
500g ricotta • ½ cup cream
250g mozzarella or goat's cheese (chevin)
80g grated Parmesan

continues on page 124…

...continued from page 123

To make the sauce, sauté the onion and garlic in olive oil until soft (about 5 minutes). Add the tomatoes, wine and sugar and season to taste. Simmer for at least 20 minutes, allowing the sauce to thicken.

For the vegetables, fry the mushrooms in olive oil until they start to caramelise. Slice the aubergine lengthways into 5mm-thick slices, brush each side with olive oil, and grill for 4 minutes on each side. Quarter the red peppers, then char-grill them directly over a hot flame or under a hot grill. Place the charred peppers into a plastic bag so they start to sweat, making them easier to peel.

Preheat the oven to 190°C. To assemble the lasagne, spread a third of the tomato sauce on the bottom of a baking dish. Then scatter – in this order – half the basil leaves, aubergine, peppers, lasagne sheets, ricotta, mushrooms and cream. Repeat, starting with the tomato sauce and ending with the last third of tomato sauce. Bake for 30 minutes.

Remove from the oven and top the lasagne with mozzarella (or goat's cheese) and Parmesan and bake for a further 10 minutes until golden brown.

butternut tagliatelle
with crispy bacon & mushrooms

This sauce is a refreshing change from the ubiquitous tomato- or cream-based varieties. I've included bacon and crispy prosciutto in this recipe, but it can just as easily be left out and replaced with a sprinkling of toasted pumpkin seeds to make it a vegetarian dish.
I like the bacon to remain crispy, so I cook it beforehand and add it again right at the end, half mixed into the sauce and half scattered over the top for a lovely crunchy texture.
I use shiitake mushrooms because I love their slightly chewy texture and meaty flavour, but any mushrooms will work well. I tend to avoid the white-button ones, though, as they don't have as much flavour as other varieties.

Serves 2

1 medium butternut, peeled and diced (about 4 heaped cups)
olive oil for drizzling · salt · freshly ground black pepper
4 slices prosciutto or Parma ham (optional)
150g mascarpone
1 cup chicken stock
100g smoked streaky bacon, finely chopped
120g shiitake or brown mushrooms, sliced
2t chopped fresh thyme
300g fresh tagliatelle or 250g dry pasta
freshly grated Parmesan, to serve

continues on page 129…

…continued from page 126

Preheat the oven to 200°C, place the butternut on a baking tray and drizzle with olive oil, coating well. Season with salt and pepper and bake for 25 to 30 minutes, or until caramelised and tender. Remove from the oven and allow to cool. While the oven is still hot, place the prosciutto or Parma ham (if using) on a baking tray and roast for 5 to 10 minutes, or until crispy and curled. Set aside.

Blend the butternut, mascarpone and stock in a food processor until smooth. Adjust the seasoning. Heat a nonstick frying pan and fry the bacon until crispy, then drain on kitchen paper. Using the same pan, sauté the mushrooms until they just start to caramelise (about 4 minutes). Add the thyme and cook for another minute or two. Add the butternut mixture to the mushrooms and stir through.

Cook the pasta in salted water until *al dente* and drain, reserving some of the cooking liquid. Add the cooked pasta and half the bacon to the butternut and stir. If the sauce is a bit thick, add about 60ml of the pasta water to thin it out. Scatter over the remaining bacon bits.

Serve with fresh Parmesan and the crispy prosciutto.

beetroot & barley 'risotto'

This healthy vegetarian dish makes a perfect weeknight supper.

Serves 2

3T olive oil, plus extra for drizzling
1 white onion, finely chopped
1 celery stalk, finely diced
250g beetroot, peeled and chopped into small chunks (about 3cm)
1 cup barley · ½ cup dry white wine
3 cups hot vegetable stock
1T balsamic vinegar · 1T finely chopped parsley
salt · freshly ground black pepper
Parmesan or pecorino shavings, to serve

Heat the olive oil in a large, heavy-based pot and gently fry the onion and
celery until just soft (about 5 minutes). Add the beetroot and toss.
Add the barley and stir well, making sure it gets coated in the oil.
Add the wine and allow to evaporate. Add 2 cups of stock,
cover and cook for about 20 minutes, stirring occasionally.

Remove the lid and gradually add the remaining stock,
allowing each addition to be absorbed before adding the next.
The barley should be tender, but still have a bit of a bite.
Add the balsamic vinegar and parsley and season to taste.
Turn off the heat, cover and allow to stand for 5 minutes.

Drizzle over a little olive oil and serve with the pecorino or Parmesan shavings.

the best-ever roast chicken

with herbs & wine

This is without a doubt my all-time favourite roast chicken recipe and comes from Justine Drake, a South African cook I admire greatly. I have used wine in the recipe, but the original uses verjuice. I have also added onions and carrots to the roasting pan. The quantity of liquid may seem excessive, but it makes the most delicious gravy; you'll be wishing there was more.

Serves 4

1 large free-range chicken or 2 baby chickens
1 onion, peeled and roughly chopped
2 carrots, peeled and roughly chopped
1 cup dry white wine or verjuice
½ cup chicken stock
1T Dijon mustard
4 cloves garlic, crushed
½ cup finely chopped herbs (rosemary, parsley, thyme and sage)
3T olive oil • salt
freshly ground black pepper

Preheat the oven to 200°C. Place the onion and carrots in a deep roasting pan – don't use one that is too big or the liquid will evaporate. Top with the chicken. Mix the wine or verjuice, stock, mustard, garlic and herbs and pour over the chicken and into the cavity of the bird/s. Drizzle over the olive oil and season. Roast uncovered for 1½ hours, or until cooked through.

chicken, sausage & potato tray bake
with marmalade & thyme

This is a no-fuss dinner option, as everything is cooked together.
Serve it with steamed green beans or asparagus.

Serves 4

3T olive oil
8 chicken pieces (bone in, with or without skin)
salt · freshly ground black pepper
½ cup dry white wine
400ml chicken stock
3T fine-cut marmalade
1½T chopped thyme
250g chipolata pork (or ordinary pork) sausages
500g new potatoes

Preheat the oven to 200°C. Heat the olive oil in a large nonstick pan.
Season the chicken pieces and fry until golden brown on both sides.
Transfer to a roasting pan deep enough to hold the liquid.
Add the wine and stock to a pot, along with the marmalade and thyme,
and heat through. Scatter the sausages and potatoes among the chicken
pieces, pour over the liquid and bake uncovered for 45 minutes.

moroccan meatballs
with herby couscous

This recipe is inspired by my love of North African flavours.
The meatballs are fragrant and spicy and the dukkah
adds a crunchy texture.

Serves 2 – 4

500g beef mince · 1 onion, grated · 1 garlic clove, crushed
a pinch dried chilli flakes · 2T dukkah · 1t ground cumin
salt · freshly ground black pepper · olive oil for frying

For the sauce
1 onion, finely chopped · 2 garlic cloves, crushed · 1t cumin
½t ground cinnamon · 1t chilli flakes
2 x 410g tins chopped peeled tomatoes · 200ml beef or lamb stock
salt · fresh coriander, to garnish

For the herby couscous
200g couscous (I prefer wholewheat) · 350ml hot chicken stock
2T olive oil (or 50g butter) · 2T chopped parsley · 2T chopped coriander

Place all the meatball ingredients, except the olive oil, in a bowl
and combine using your hands. Roll into balls (I prefer making them
small, as they are easier to fry). Heat the olive oil in a nonstick pan and
fry the meatballs in batches until nicely browned on all sides. Set aside.

To make the sauce, lightly fry the onion, garlic and spices in the same pan
used for the meatballs, then add the tomatoes and stock. Bring to the boil,
then reduce the heat and simmer for 10 minutes, or until slightly thickened.
Season to taste. Add the meatballs to the pan and cook for 8 to 10 minutes.

To make the couscous, place it in a bowl and pour over the stock and olive oil.
Cover tightly and allow to stand until all the water has been absorbed.
Fluff up with a fork and mix in the freshly chopped herbs.

To serve, top the couscous with a generous helping of
meatballs and sauce. Garnish with fresh coriander.

rustic lamb pie

This wonderfully comforting dish is ideal for feeding a crowd.
You could make it using the lamb-shank ragout recipe
(page 118), but you would need to increase the quantity of lamb
shanks to 4 (roughly 2kg) to make a more meaty and less saucy
base for the pie. You could also use 1.5kg cubed leg of lamb
and cook it in the same way as you would the shanks.
If you are using just the meat, reduce the cooking time
to 3½ hours. If you want to make a smaller pie, use less meat
and reduce the amount of stock so that it just covers the meat.

Serves 6 – 8

4 lamb shanks (about 2kg), cooked according to the
lamb-shank ragout recipe on page 118
4 large potatoes • 4T melted butter
½ cup cream • fresh rosemary
salt • freshly ground black pepper

Preheat the oven to 180°C. Spread the cooked meat out in a casserole dish.
Peel and slice the potatoes very thinly (I find a mandolin on a narrow setting
works very well) and layer some over the meat. Brush each layer of potato
with melted butter and drizzle over a thin layer of cream before adding the
next layer. You should be able to make 3 to 4 layers. Brush the top layer
with butter and scatter over fresh rosemary, salt and pepper to taste. Bake
for 40 to 50 minutes, or until the crust is golden brown and cooked through.

Serve with steamed green beans or peas,
or any other vegetable of your choice.

apple galettes
with salted caramel

The flavour combination of apple and salted caramel, my two favourites, is absolutely sublime. Any leftover caramel can be spooned over ice cream or just eaten straight out of the jar.

Serves 4 – 8

For the pastry
¾ cups (120g) cake flour + extra for dusting
¾ cup (120g) wholewheat flour
a pinch salt
170g butter, cut into small cubes
⅓ cup ice-cold water

For the filling
3 apples, cored and sliced into thin wedges
4T brown sugar
1t ground cinnamon
2T melted butter

For the salted caramel
200g sugar
80g butter, cut into small cubes
½ cup cream
a pinch sea salt flakes

Using a food processor, briefly mix the flours and salt.
Add the butter and pulse until the mix resembles breadcrumbs.
Add the water and pulse until the dough just comes together (do not overmix).
Divide the dough into four equal portions and roll out into rough circles
on a floured surface. (Using a chilled bottle of water or wine
for rolling is useful, as it keeps the pastry cool.)

continues on page 142…

…continued from page 141

To make the pastry

Place the pastry rounds on a baking tray lined with baking paper.
Toss the apple slices with the sugar and cinnamon and arrange
them in a fan in the centre of each pastry round, leaving a little
space around the edge of each pie. Fold the edges of the pastry
inwards. Brush the upturned edges of each one with melted butter.
Chill in the fridge while you preheat the oven to 200°C. Bake for
45 minutes, loosely covering the tarts with foil about 20 minutes
into the baking time to prevent overbrowning.

To make the salted caramel, dissolve the sugar in
a heavy-based pot. (Be extremely cautious here, as molten sugar
can burn you if it comes in contact with your skin.)
As soon as the sugar has dissolved, remove it from the heat.
Add the butter in parts while whisking continuously.
Return the pot to the heat and add the cream, still whisking vigorously.

When the sauce is smooth and well-combined, remove it from
the heat, add a pinch of salt and stir to dissolve.
Allow it to cool completely, then stir in another sprinkle of salt
but do not let it dissolve – the crunchiness adds texture.
Taste it and add more salt if desired.

To serve, drizzle the salted caramel over the warm apple tarts.

Cook's notes Leftover salted caramel
can be stored in sterilised jars for weeks.

orange malva pudding

This pudding should actually be called 'death by butter'. Quintessentially South African, it is the perfect end to an evening feast. I substitute the water for orange juice, which gives a wonderful citrus flavour.

Serves 4 – 6

1 large free-range egg · 1 cup sugar · 1T smooth apricot jam
1 cup flour · 1t bicarbonate of soda
a pinch salt · 1t butter, melted
1t vinegar · 1 cup milk

For the sauce
¾ cup cream · 110g butter
¾ cup sugar · 100ml orange juice
cream or custard, to serve

Preheat the oven to 180°C. Using an electric mixer, beat the egg, sugar and jam on a high speed for about 5 minutes. In a separate bowl, sift the flour, bicarbonate of soda and salt.

Mix the melted butter with the vinegar.
Gradually add the milk and flour alternately to the egg mixture until well combined, then add the butter-and-vinegar mixture.
Pour the batter into an appropriately sized greased baking dish, cover with foil and bake for 45 minutes, or until golden brown.

While the pudding is baking, heat the sauce ingredients in a pot over a medium heat until the butter has melted and the sugar dissolved. Pour the sauce over the pudding as soon as it comes out of the oven. It may appear as if there is too much sauce, but the pudding will eventually absorb it.

Serve it with cream or custard.

mini pavlovas
with mango purée & raspberries

I use a meringue recipe for this wonderful summer dessert
instead of a pavlova recipe – increasing the size of the meringues
and decreasing the cooking time. You want to achieve a thin,
crispy outer layer and a soft but firm centre. The meringues can be
made in advance and stored in an airtight container until needed.

Makes 5 – 6

4 large free-range egg whites (at room temperature)
1 cup sugar · 1t white vinegar
2t cornflour · 2 ripe mangoes
1T icing sugar (optional)
vanilla ice cream (or whipped cream) and fresh raspberries, to serve

Preheat the oven to 150°C. Beat the egg whites with an electric
beater until they form stiff peaks. With the mixer still running on
medium speed, very gradually add the sugar (over about two minutes),
and then beat the mixture on high speed for 4 to 5 minutes
until glossy. Sift the cornflour and stir the vinegar into
the mixture, folding through by hand.

Line a baking tray with baking paper (or use a nonstick plastic baking sheet)
and dollop the meringue mixture onto the tray in your desired size.
Shape using a small spatula or spoon.

Place the tray in the oven and immediately reduce the temperature
to 120°C and bake for 25 to 30 minutes. Turn off the oven and
allow the meringues to cool completely. You could bake them
for a little longer if you want a crispier texture.

To make the mango purée, blend the mangoes in a food processor until
smooth. I don't add any sugar here as I like the slight acidity of the fruit with
the sweet meringue, but you can add the icing sugar if you want to.

To serve, top the meringue with a scoop of vanilla ice cream
or freshly whipped cream, then pour over the
mango purée and top with fresh raspberries.

cherry & oat
apple crumble

The ultimate comfort food, a traditional apple crumble
is given a new lease with the addition of cherries and oats.

Serves 4 – 6

150g flour
100g brown sugar
150g butter
70g oats
vanilla ice cream or cream, to serve

For the filling
2 x 350g tins pie apple slices
300g fresh or frozen cherries (thawed)
1½t cinnamon
7T brown sugar + 1T for sprinkling

Preheat the oven to 180°C. Briefly blend the flour, sugar and butter
in a food processor until it forms loose crumbs. You could also use
your fingers to do this. Add the oats and mix by hand – don't worry
if there are a few clumps. Mix the filling ingredients and place in
a 25cm pie dish. Spread the crumble mixture evenly over the
top and sprinkle over the sugar for extra crunch.
Bake for 30 to 40 minutes, or until golden brown.

Serve with a scoop of vanilla ice cream or fresh cream.

milk chocolate
& horlicks ice cream
with cape velvet & hot-chocolate sauce

The chocolate in the ice cream is quite subtle so the
rich, dark sauce makes the perfect accompaniment.
With the liqueur, this is a decadent adult dessert…

Makes about 1 litre

1 cup milk · 50g Horlicks
100g milk chocolate, broken into pieces
2 large free-range eggs · ½ cup sugar · 2 cups cream
2T Cape Velvet or Baileys liqueur (optional)

For the chocolate sauce
100g good-quality dark chocolate (preferably 70%)
¼ cup cream
1T Cape Velvet or Baileys liqueur (optional)

Heat the milk and Horlicks in a saucepan over a medium heat.
Add the chocolate and stir until melted. Do not allow the milk to boil.
Remove from the heat and cool. Using an electric beater, beat the eggs
until light and fluffy (about 2 minutes), then slowly add the sugar
and continue beating for another minute or so. Add the cooled
chocolate mixture, cream and liqueur and mix briefly to combine. Process
in an ice cream machine according to the manufacturer's instructions.

To make the chocolate sauce, melt all the ingredients in a
double-boiler and serve warm over the ice cream.

cook's notes

The recipes in this book are a mix of metric and cup measurements
and are given as accurately as possible, but I do encourage you
to use them as a guideline and adapt where you see fit. It's the way
I approach cooking – adding a little extra of this or less of that is all
part of the fun and creative process.

The baking recipes require a stricter approach, so I've included
a conversion table on the opposite page to help you with
the measurements that might be more familiar to you.

All oven temperatures are for a conventional oven.
If you are using a convection (fan) oven you will need to
adjust the temperature by around 20°C (lower).

I've abbreviated teaspoons to 't' and tablespoons to 'T' throughout.

All eggs are large and always free range and for everything else,
and where possible, source the best-quality ingredients you can afford.
It makes the world of difference. What you put in is what you get out
– it's as simple as that.

If you have any specific questions about any of my recipes
please contact me via www.drizzleanddip.com.
I'd love to hear from you.

conversion table

Weight

Metric	Imperial
15g	½ oz
30g	1 oz
60g	2 oz
90g	3 oz
125g	4 oz
175g	6 oz
250g	8 oz
300g	10 oz
375g	12 oz
400g	13 oz
425g	14 oz
500g	1 lb
750g	1½ lb
1kg	2 lb

Length

Metric	Imperial
5mm	¼ inch
1cm	½ inch
2.5cm	1 inch
5cm	2 inches
7cm	3 inches
10cm	4 inches
12cm	5 inches
15cm	6 inches
18cm	7 inches
20cm	8 inches
23cm	9 inches
25cm	10 inches
28cm	11 inches
30cm	12 inches

Liquid measures

Quantity	Metric
1 teaspoon (1t)	5ml
1 tablespoon (1T)	15ml
¼ cup	60ml
⅓ cup	80ml
½ cup	125ml
⅔ cup	160ml
¾ cup	180ml
1 cup	250ml
1¼ cups	300ml
1½ cups	375ml
1⅔ cups	400ml
1¾ cups	450ml
2 cups	500ml
2½ cups	600ml
3 cups	750ml

Oven temperature

Celsius	Fahrenheit
110°C	225°F
120°C	250°F
140°C	275°F
150°C	300°F
160°C	325°F
180°C	350°F
190°C	375°F
200°C	400°F
220°C	425°F
230°C	450°F

To my mom Sally

I will always love you. I wish you were here to see what I have done. This book is dedicated to you and to your love. Thank you for encouraging and nurturing my early interest in cooking and baking – it's at times like these that I miss you the most.

Thanks

My journey of writing my food blog has often been a lonely one, but putting this book together has been the opposite.

Thank you to my friends and family for all the love and support you have given me on this sometimes rocky road, and to everyone who has offered me a kind word of encouragement as I doubted myself so many times.

As this book was born out of my food blog Drizzle & Dip, I have to thank all the readers and friends of my website without whose support I could not have written this book.

A very big and special thank you to: Dad and Marie for the love and inspiration, always. To Grant for taking on this publishing project and calmly guiding me through this unfamiliar territory. To Nikki for editing my words and pulling them into shape and teaching me about consistency. To Christoff for your design and layout. To Tim for editing my images and Micky for taking the pictures of me. To my sister Anthea for designing such a lovely cover. To Paul for nudging me towards this. To Michael for your ongoing support and encouragement, it has meant the world to me. To Kristy for your help and support. To Laeni for proofreading this book. To Anne, David, Pete, Elize, Clare, Vivian and Sonia for your pearls of wisdom along the way and to Laurence, Justine and Kirsten for so generously sharing your recipes. To Lori and Laurence for your support from the beginning, for being my foodie sounding boards and such good friends of Drizzle & Dip.

Published by Eat the Book

Publishing Consultants: Schreiber Media
www.schreibermedia.net

First published 2012

Publication © 2012 Eat the Book
Text and photographs © 2012 Samantha Linsell

All rights reserved. No part of this publication may be
reproduced, stored in any retrieval system or transmitted,
in any form or by any means, electronic, mechanical,
photocopying, recording or otherwise, without prior written
permission of the copyright owners.

Concept, recipes, photography & styling
Samantha Linsell

Publishing editor Grant Schreiber
Art director Christoff van Wyk
Copy editor Nikki Benatar
Picture editor Timothy Atkins
Cover design Anthea Linsell
Author's photograph Micky Hoyle
Proofreader Laeni Gittins-Spiers

Printing Craft Print International Limited
Distribution & marketing Jacana Media

ISBN 978-0-620-53074-3
www.eatthebook.co.za

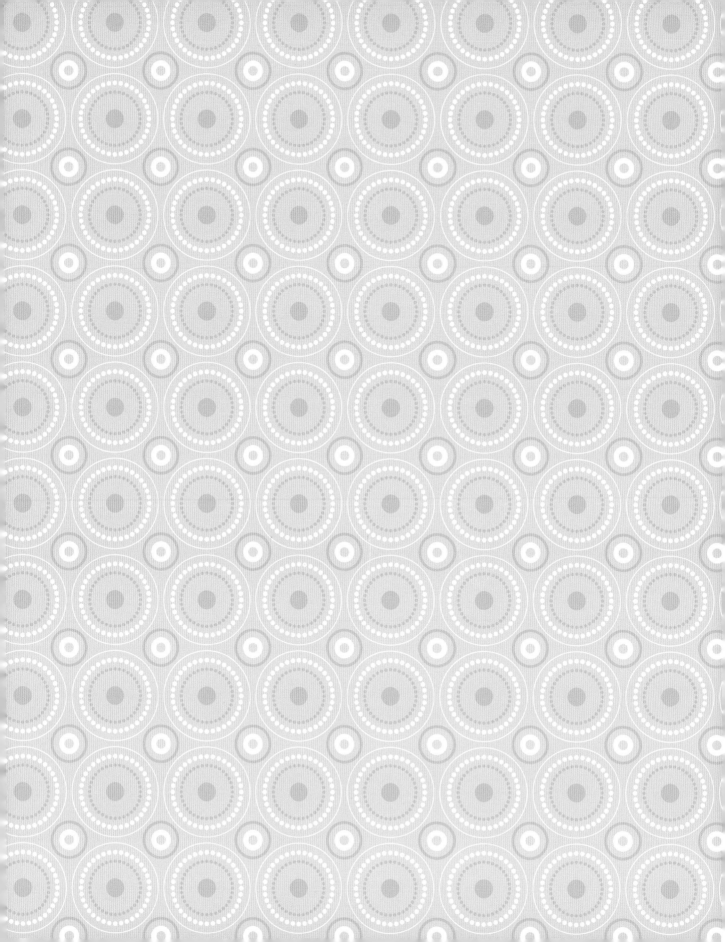

eat the book